Hallmarks of Effective Outcomes Assessment

Edited by Trudy W. Banta

**Assessment
UPdate**
COLLECTIONS

Contents

Introduction:
What Are Some Hallmarks of
Effective Practice in Assessment?

Trudy W. Banta

How do I get started in assessing outcomes? How can I convince my colleagues that they should get involved in assessment? What methods should we use? Once begun, how can we sustain our assessment initiatives?

These questions are asked by faculty, staff, and administrators on campuses across the country every day. And they will continue to be asked as long as there is a college, a department, or a program that has not yet adopted strategies for collecting credible evidence of the progress they are making in attaining their goals for student growth, development, and success and using that evidence to improve their academic programs and student services continuously.

Unfortunately there is no silver bullet, no magic potion, no single step-by-step approach that will provide easy answers to the fundamental questions about how to get started in outcomes assessment. This is because every setting is different and requires its own unique approach, taking into account the mission and goals of the campus and of the individual unit undertaking assessment, the expertise and interests of those to be involved in achieving the mission and goals and in guiding assessment, the prior history of evaluation initiatives in the unit, and the resources available to implement assessment, to name just a few of the relevant variables.

Fortunately there is some guidance that pioneers and experienced practitioners in assessment have assembled over the years, and the articles in this volume of *Collections* have been selected because they illustrate this body of work.

In the early 1990s a group of a dozen assessment scholars began to meet periodically under the auspices of the American Association for Higher Education. In 1992 that group completed a brief statement entitled "Principles of Good Practice for Assessing Student Learning" and we published those principles in *Assessment Update* in an article by the leader of the AAHE initiative, Pat Hutchings. In 1996 my colleagues Jon Lund, Karen Black, and Frances Oblander joined me in producing a volume that illustrates the nine AAHE principles, plus a tenth principle added by these authors, with examples gleaned from 165 cases submitted by assessment practitioners from across the country. Over the next five years others, including the American Productivity and Quality Center (1998) and Jones, Voorhees, and Paulson (2001), added principles of good practice to the assessment literature. In 2002 I drew on all these sources to develop a list of seventeen hallmarks I called "Characteristics of Effective Outcomes Assessment" that I will use now to provide some context for the articles selected for this issue.

I wish it were possible to say that there is a first step everyone should take as they contemplate an approach to assessment. My suggestion for that step would be to lay out a multi-year plan for assessment that takes the campus or department mission into account and uses the particular resources, including faculty expertise, that are available. But I have observed successful programs that simply began with a collection of data— giving a standardized test or administering a questionnaire—and took up the issue of multi-year planning later.

So the best I can do is characterize effective practice in assessment and suggest that the reader find the best place to enter the sequence. My hallmarks cluster in three phases—*planning, implementing,* and *improving and sustaining* assessment. A matrix at the end of this introduction will direct you to the articles that best illustrate particular characteristics.

Effective assessment *planning:*

- Involves stakeholders (faculty members, administrators, students, student affairs professionals, employers, community representatives) from the outset to incorporate their needs and interests and to solicit later support.

- Begins when the need is recognized; allows sufficient time for development. Timing is crucial.
- Has a written plan with clear purposes that is related to goals people value—to a larger set of conditions that promote change. Assessment is a vehicle for improvement, not an end in itself.
- Bases assessment approaches on clear, explicitly stated program objectives.

A very few institutions, like Alverno College, have undertaken assessment for their own purposes: seeking credible evidence that their programs and services are as effective as they can be in promoting student growth and development and using their assessment findings to make warranted improvements. But most colleges and universities have been influenced to begin the assessment process by the necessity of responding to an external requirement—a state or governing board mandate or self-study guidelines imposed by an accrediting body, as illustrated by the article in this booklet by Santiago. If assessment is not to become a perfunctory response designed merely to fulfill the minimum requirements of an external mandate, it must engage those who need to be involved. Much more than a directive from the president or academic dean is needed, though support at these levels is essential. Students, faculty and staff, parents and alumni, employers and community members are the stakeholders in higher education and the more deeply these groups are engaged in outcomes assessment, the more meaningful, effective, and sustained that process will be. The articles in this issue by Santiago, Banta, Nelson, Cavanaugh, Madison, and Haessig provide examples of the ways in which stakeholders can contribute effectively in making assessment meaningful and productive.

As Peter Gray's article shows, stakeholders are much more likely to become engaged if they can perceive assessment as an integral part of a process they value such as curriculum development, peer review, or personal scholarship. Articles by Banta, Haessig, and Smith illustrate how timing is important. For example, at the time that a major curricular change is to be introduced, program graduates and employers may be invited to comment on the effectiveness of the prior curriculum and to suggest new student outcomes that are desirable from their perspective. Faculty will have an interest in learning whether the new curriculum they develop is more effective than the one it replaces and assessment can be introduced at this point as the tool that provides the evidence of that effectiveness.

A good program will be guided by a plan that begins with clearly stated goals and objectives, as illustrated by seven articles in this booklet. In the academy, programs should be based on the outcomes for student learning and development that faculty (and other stakeholders) believe to be important. If objectives are stated in terms of what students should know and be able to do, using action verbs, it will be relatively easy to see what assessment measures are most appropriate. That is, if we say that students should be able to make an effective oral presentation, then the assessment method should incorporate a graded oral presentation.

In addition to specific objectives and multiple measures, a plan for assessment should include a timetable, a practice that is well illustrated by five of the articles. It is neither feasible in terms of people's time and other resources nor necessary to use every assessment tool every semester, or even every year. But there should be a schedule for applying every relevant measure over a period of years.

Effective *implementation* of assessment:

- Has knowledgeable, effective leadership.
- Involves recognition that assessment is essential to learning, and therefore is everyone's responsibility.
- Includes faculty and staff development to prepare individuals to implement assessment and use the findings.
- Devolves responsibility for assessment to the unit level.
- Recognizes that learning is multidimensional and developmental and thus uses multiple measures, therefore maximizing reliability and validity.
- Assesses processes as well as outcomes.

Leadership for assessment must emanate from the highest levels in an institution, but it also must come from faculty, librarians, and student affairs professionals. The responsibility for advancing student learning, and the assessment thereof, is everyone's responsibility. An assessment coordinator, advised by a broadly representative group of academics and administrators, provides the most powerful leadership team. There are numerous articles illustrating this principle, such as the one by Cavanaugh.

Most faculty are not trained as teachers, and even those who are often feel inadequate when confronted with the challenge of assessing student learning. Librarians and student affairs staff also express concern about their ability to assess the perceived value and success of their programs. Thus faculty and staff need to attend conferences off campus, workshops on campus, and engage in joint reviews and discussion of relevant literature in order to develop their knowledge and skills in assessment, as described by Santiago, Banta, Madison, and Haessig.

Assessment of learning begins with one student in a single class. Looking across the work of individuals in a single class, a faculty member can assess learning strengths and weaknesses that suggest where instructional strategies have been particularly successful or unsuccessful. Faculty in a department can discuss evidence about strengths and weaknesses in student learning across sections of the same course or courses that constitute a curriculum for majors. Assessment data can be aggregated across majors and across academic units to draw conclusions about the effectiveness of college- or institution-wide initiatives. But data collected and interpreted at the classroom or department level will most often produce constructive change because they are perceived to be of immediate relevance to those who are in the best position to act on them.

Direct measures of student learning such as assignments, tests, and projects must be supplemented by indirect measures like questionnaires, interviews, and focus groups. Direct measures reveal *what* students know and can do, but it takes indirect measures to suggest *why* performance was above or below expectations and what might be done to improve the processes of education. Multiple measures are essential because no single measure is perfectly reliable or valid; several measures of the same construct can furnish support for one another as stakeholders draw conclusions about strengths or weaknesses (see all of the articles for examples of assessment methods).

Effective practice in *improving and sustaining* assessment:

- Produces credible evidence of learning and organizational effectiveness.
- Is undertaken in an environment that is receptive; supportive; and enabling—on a continuing basis.
- Incorporates continuous communications with constituents concerning activities and findings. Effective outcomes assessment produces data that guide *improvement* on a continuing basis.
- Ensures that assessment data are used continuously to improve programs and services.
- Provides a vehicle for demonstrating accountability to stakeholders within and outside the institution.
- Encompasses the expectation that outcomes assessment will be ongoing, not episodic. Recognizes and celebrates successes and those who contribute to them.
- Incorporates ongoing evaluation and improvement of the assessment process itself.

Many colleges and universities aspire to create "a culture of evidence"—an environment in which important decisions are based on the study of relevant data. This culture is attainable only if the data produced have credibility with the faculty and staff who must rely upon them. Through the engagement of stakeholders in the design and conduct of assessment, trust in the process can be built and credibility of the findings can be established. Top administrators and faculty and staff leaders can provide support and thus produce an environment for assessment that is receptive, supportive, and enabling.

Credibility is enhanced and motivation to use assessment findings is stimulated if findings are interpreted and disseminated in reports that make sense to potential users (see Santiago, Gray, Morey, Juillerat, and Smith).

While it is important to use assessment data to demonstrate accountability to external audiences, there can be no culture of evidence unless assessment data are utilized on a continuing basis to guide internal institutional improvement in programs and services (see Santiago, Nelson, Cavanaugh, Morey, Juillerat, and Smith).

An effective plan for assessment charts a multi-year course. Assessment must be ongoing, not episodic, disappearing from the institutional agenda once the state report has been submitted or notice of reaccreditation received. An important element in sustaining assessment is recognizing and rewarding those who contribute their time and talents to it (see Santiago, Morey, and Haessig). And finally, an unexamined assessment program can become stagnant; periodic peer review should be scheduled to refresh the process (see Santiago).

References

American Productivity and Quality Center. *Benchmarking Best Practices in Assessing Learning Outcomes: Final Report.* Houston, TX. American Productivity and Quality Center, 1998.

Banta, T. W. "Characteristics of Effective Outcomes Assessment." In Banta, T. W., and Associates. *Building a Scholarship of Assessment.* San Francisco: Jossey-Bass, 2002.

Banta, T.W., Lund, J. P., Black, K. E., and Oblander, F. W. *Assessment in Practice: Putting Principles to Work on College Campuses.* San Francisco: Jossey-Bass, 1996.

Hutchings, P. "Principles of Good Practice for Assessing Student Learning." *Assessment Update,* 1993, 5(1), 6–7.

Jones, E. A., Voorhees, R. A., Paulson, K. *Defining and Assessing Learning: Exploring Competence-Based Initiatives. A Report of the National Post Secondary Education Cooperative.* Washington, D.C.: U.S. Department of Education, National Center for Education Statistics, 2001.

Matrix: Hallmarks of Effective Practice

HALLMARKS	Santiago	Banta	Nelson	Cavanagh	Forest	Gray	Haessig	Madison	Morey	Juillerat	Smith
Planning:											
A. External Influences	✔						✔				✔
B. Engaging Stakeholders	✔	✔	✔	✔			✔				✔
C. Focus on Goals		✔	✔	✔	✔	✔			✔		✔
D. Developing a Plan	✔			✔		✔		✔	✔		
E. Time		✔					✔				✔
Implementing:											
F. Methods	✔	✔	✔	✔	✔	✔	✔	✔	✔	✔	✔
G. Faculty Development	✔	✔					✔	✔			
H. Leadership				✔	✔	✔	✔	✔	✔		
Sustaining:											
I. Interpreting Findings	✔									✔	
J. Reporting Results	✔					✔			✔		✔
K. Using Results	✔		✔	✔					✔	✔	✔
L. Recognizing Success	✔						✔		✔		
M. Improving Assessment	✔										

Institution-Wide Approaches

Toward Excellence in Outcomes Assessment: The Middle States Approach

George Santiago, Jr.

What do excellent institution-wide assessment plans look like? The Middle States Commission, which has been working in numerous ways to help raise the standard of outcomes assessment, identified fifteen institutions with exemplary assessment plans. Here is a summary of many of those plans, as well as a general discussion of the efforts of the Middle States Commission. From Assessment Update 13:5. For a listing of hallmarks illustrated in this article see the matrix on page 8.

Regional accreditors in the United States have reached a consensus that the accreditation process should increase the attention given to outcomes assessment and learning outcomes in particular (McMurtrie, 2000), not only in campus-based programs but in distance education as well (Carnevale, 2000). The Middle States Commission on Higher Education, implementing this consensus, is collaborating with its other regional colleagues to reinforce the significance of outcomes in its own evaluation process, provide technical assistance to member institutions, and revise its standards for accreditation.

Developing and implementing institution-wide outcomes assessment plans present numerous challenges to both regional accrediting agencies and institutions. For regional associations, these challenges include defining standards that are meaningful to institutions and relevant to their current contexts and providing learning opportunities to institutions on how to develop and implement assessment plans. For institutions, challenges include creating a culture of assessment on campus, reallocating resources to support long-term assessment initiatives, overcoming faculty resistance, and resolving questions of administration and governance.

Revising Standards

The commission's standards for accreditation, *Characteristics of Excellence in Higher Education*, are a guide for institutions considering applying for membership, those accepted as candidate institutions, and accredited institutions engaged in self-review and peer evaluation (Middle States Commission on Higher Education, 1994). Proposed revisions to *Characteristics of Excellence* are scheduled to be published in 2002 after the commission receives comment from members, candidates, and other colleagues in higher education.

The new edition will differ from prior editions in both emphasis and format. Among the principles that guided the development of these revised standards, three are particularly noteworthy. First, these standards consistently emphasize student learning and student learning outcomes. Second, the standards acknowledge the diversity of educational delivery systems that enable institutions to meet accreditation standards. And third, in order to achieve greater specificity, the standards are more clearly defined and illustrated, including examples of evidence that could substantiate an institution's achievement of the standards.

The emphasis on student learning and student learning outcomes follows naturally from the commission's existing standards and decades of attention to outcomes assessment through publications, workshops, and training sessions. Nonetheless, the commission is mindful of the institutional effort and cultural change that the increased emphasis on student learning outcomes may require.

The commission acknowledges that in order to meet these revised standards, institutions will be called upon to commit resources to the tasks of research and analysis, particularly as related to the assessment and improvement of teaching and learning. Concurrently, there is an understanding that in the changing environment of higher education, there is much that warrants further research and study.

These standards also affirm that the individual mission and goals of each institution remain the context within which these accreditation standards are applied during self-study and evaluation. The standards emphasize functions rather than specific structures, recognizing that there are many models for educational excellence.

Technical Assistance to Institutions

Since 1999, the Middle States Commission has included an outcomes assessment resource person on each evaluation team. The role of this person is to evaluate an institution's comprehensive outcomes assessment plan and to assist other team members in framing outcomes assessment questions in specific areas such as general education, academic programs, distance learning, student services, and library and learning resources. A number of strategies have been employed to identify and train the number of individuals needed to support this initiative.

In addition to training new evaluators, the commission continues to provide its member institutions with technical assistance through symposia, conferences, and workshops on various topics of special interest to the commission. It has expanded its Web site <http://www.msache.org> to include best practices in assessment, and a new initiative is being developed on learning outcomes.

Though outcomes assessment has been explicit in Middle States standards for decades, intensive conferences on the subject began in 1996. In spring 2000, the Middle States Commission convened two conferences on outcomes assessment and accreditation: one in Philadelphia and one in San Juan, Puerto Rico, where the Middle States Commission currently has 43 member institutions. These conferences offered broad-based, hands-on learning experiences on how to conduct outcomes assessment at an institution as well as how to frame outcomes assessment questions in such areas as general education, student affairs, distance education, and library and learning resources. Approximately 500 participants attended these two conferences.

Exemplary Institutional Plans

During summer 2000, the commission's senior staff and several consultants from member institutions reviewed self-study reports from institutions that had completed their decennial evaluations recently, as well as periodic review reports that are submitted during the fifth year of the evaluation cycle. A number of exemplary comprehensive outcomes assessment plans or components of plans were identified. This review was guided by the criteria for assessment plans published in *Outcomes Assessment Plans* (Middle States Commission on Higher Education, 1998), a commission guide for institutions and evaluators. The criteria for plans include a foundation in the institution's mission, goals, and objectives; the support and collaboration of faculty and administration; a systematic and thorough use of quantitative and qualitative measures; assessment and evaluative approaches that lead to improvement; realistic goals and a timetable, supported by appropriate investment; and an evaluation of the assessment program.

Fifteen institutions that demonstrate an exemplary plan or components of a plan were selected in this first cycle of continuing review. The institutions are American Academy of the Dramatic Arts, Carlos Albizu University, Cecil Community College, Elizabethtown College, King's College, Mercy College, Middlesex County College, Nassau Community College, St. Mary's College of Maryland, St. John's College in Maryland, SUNY at Albany, SUNY-College at Fredonia, SUNY Empire State College, SUNY Institute of Technology at Utica/Rome, and Towson University. Three examples of their approaches to assessment follow.

• The King's College model of assessment focuses on (1) clearly defined faculty expectations for learning that students can understand; (2) explicit criteria that faculty and students can use to evaluate performance; (3) clear, honest, and timely feedback to students so that they can concentrate not so much on past mistakes as on practical ways to improve performance; (4) strategies to enable students to connect learning in the Core curriculum with learning in the major; (5) close collaboration, a helping relationship, between faculty and students, to encourage ongoing development; and (6) students understanding more of what and how they learn so that they can become more involved in their learning and more responsible for that learning. The King's assessment program includes pre- and post-assessments in Core curriculum courses, competence growth plans for the skills of liberal learning, a sophomore/junior diagnostic project, and a senior integrated assessment.

• Nassau Community College, with the leadership of the Assessment Committee of the Academic Senate, published a manual to aid faculty in their quest to discover ways to help students learn more effectively through discipline inquiries into teaching and learning in their classrooms. The manual is divided into five sections. Section One, "Introduction and Historical Perspectives," addresses the vision and evolution of assessment at the institution. Section Two, "The Conceptual Framework of Assessment," examines course-embedded assessment and the five steps of the goals-based assessment paradigm (teaching goals, outcomes behaviors, assessment measurements, evaluating measurement results, and formulating modifications). Section Three, "Implementation and Campus Process," discusses the three phases of classroom assessment (planning, implementing, and responding) and various roles of faculty, administrators, and committees at the institution. Section Four, "Classroom Assessment User's Guide," serves as a pragmatic, quick reference to methods involved in formulating classroom assessment. And Section Five, "Resource Guide," addresses the teaching goals inventory, outcomes of general education, and classroom assessment techniques.

• St. John's College in Maryland uses the great books of the Western tradition "to achieve a critical knowledge of the tradition of freedom and equality." The program is a required, nondepartmental, nonspecialized curriculum, consisting through all four years of equal parts of Great Books seminars; language study in Greek, French, and English; mathematics; and laboratory science. St. John's College employs many nontraditional assessment methods:

- Assessment meetings: Twice a year, students and tutor-teachers come together to discuss the student's total performance and the tutor's teaching.
- The enabling procedure: At the end of the sophomore year, each of a given student's tutors for the past two years reviews the student's class work and grade record and recommends to the Instruction Committee that the student continue or not continue.
- Oral examination: All students undergo a half-hour examination on books read or essays written.
- Annual essays and papers: Each spring, students are required to write a major annual paper, which is graded.
- Senior essays: A satisfactory senior essay—a substantial piece of writing—is required for graduation.
- College examination: An algebra test is required during the sophomore year.
- Graduation review: The whole faculty reviews each student prior to graduation; deficiencies must be corrected before the baccalaureate is conferred.
- Classroom preparation, participation, signs of intellectual growth, and attendance are reviewed.

The Middle States Commission will share these and other outcomes assessment initiatives from members of the Middle States community and others through its Web site at <http://www.msache.org>. The site includes a one-page description of an outcomes assessment plan (or components of a plan) and a contact person for each institution. The site is updated three times each year to coincide with the commission's review of self-studies, periodic review reports, and any follow-up reports that the commission may require institutions to provide.

The Millennium Initiative

The relationships among learning outcomes in the core disciplines, general education, and information literacy are the focus of a new initiative, Learning Outcomes in the Millennium.

Small planning meetings were held in 2000 to design local activities intended to stimulate campus dialogues on learning outcomes. They recognize the possibility of eight microregions within Middle States and follow the commission's advice to staff to take more workshops into the field, closer to member institutions. Larger workshops are planned for 2001, culminating in one or more regional conferences in 2002.

Commission staff have sent library directors in the region a survey and a concept paper on the Millennium Initiative. The survey asked library directors to identify instructional librarians, faculty members, and administrative staff involved in information literacy programs on their campuses. The survey also collected data on two major types of information literacy instruction, which led to a list of the "top ten" disciplines—those having the largest number of institutions with information literacy programs in those disciplines.

Representatives from the "top four," representing institutions where the greatest progress has been made, have been invited to Millennium Initiative planning meetings. The objective is to identify and build on these institutions' successful strategies, which can be offered as suggestions to others in the coming years.

The Middle States Commission and its staff understand their own challenges in a rapidly changing landscape of higher education. These include balancing the institutional context and the pressures from various external constituents. Using a blend of traditional and innovative techniques and strategies, Middle States has embraced its role in the assessment movement and used it as an opportunity to revise its policies and practices, educate its member institutions, and in the process, improve the manner in which it conducts business.

References

Carnevale, D. "Accrediting Bodies Consider New Standards for Distance-Education Programs." *Chronicle of Higher Education*, Sept. 8, 2000, p. A58.

McMurtrie, B., "Accreditors Revamp Policies to Stress Student Learning." *Chronicle of Higher Education*, July 7, 2000, p. A29.

Middle States Commission on Higher Education. *Characteristics of Excellence in Higher Education*. Middle States Commission on Higher Education, Philadelphia, 1994.

Middle States Commission on Higher Education. *Outcomes Assessment Plans: Guidelines for Developing Outcomes Assessment Plans at Colleges and Universities*, Middle States Commission on Higher Education, Philadelphia, 1998.

George Santiago, Jr., is executive associate director of the Middle States Commission on Higher Education.

The Syracuse Model: A Collaborative Approach to Assessment

Ronald C. Cavanagh, Franklin P. Wilbur, Peter J. Gray

This article, describing assessment at Syracuse University, shows how assessment can emerge in a meaningful way from an institution's mission, engage stakeholders on all levels, and have a meaningful effect on the institution. From Assessment Update 13:5. For a listing of hallmarks illustrated in this article see the matrix on page 8.

Assessment at Syracuse University (SU) began in the early 1990s with the arrival of Chancellor Kenneth A. Shaw. As part of his initial analysis of the campus culture, Shaw identified the five core values that characterize an education at Syracuse University: quality, caring, diversity, innovation, and service. In his first year, he launched a variety of initiatives intended to move the campus forward in relation to these core values, one of which was the development of a student learning outcomes assessment program. At the same time, the mission and vision of the university were being redefined in light of the core values, and a total quality management program was initiated for professional and administrative staff.

The mission statement, which previously had been several pages long, was refined to one line: "to promote learning through teaching, research, scholarship, creative accomplishment and service." This was followed by a fresh vision statement whose opening phrase contained the four key words (student-centered research university) that defined the university's transformation: "to be a leading student-centered research university, with faculty, students and staff sharing responsibility and working together for academic, professional and personal growth." (For more information on the student-centered research university, its development, and the activities associated with it, please see <http://www.syr.edu/acadaff>.)

The total quality management program, called Syracuse University Improving Quality (SUIQ), was designed to help some 3,000 SU staff and administrators infuse the core values into their daily operations. Faculty members were not involved in the SUIQ program, because it was clear that many of its concepts, borrowed from business and industry, were not appropriate for the context of teaching and learning. However, from the beginning, the assessment program at SU was faculty-driven. The person who chaired the committee charged with the initial formulation of the assessment program was a faculty member who also was an associate vice chancellor for academic affairs. All the chairs of the committee responsible for developing the SU assessment program over the last ten years have been senior faculty members. And the vice president for undergraduate studies has administrative responsibility for assessment at SU.

Another basic characteristic of assessment at SU is that it is collaborative. A mix of faculty, academic administrators and staff, students, and student affairs staff served on the initial organizing committee. The primary result of their efforts was a description of the guiding principles of assessment at Syracuse University that emphasized the formative, faculty-led nature of assessment. Most important, the assessment of student learning was seen as a process of continuous improvement akin to the SUIQ process but relevant to the academic enterprise. This process is intended to address the following questions: What are our hopes for our students? What are we doing to realize those hopes? How do we know if our hopes are being realized? In light of our hopes and observations both in and outside the classroom, what might we change or improve upon to realize our hopes?

Over the last ten years, the SU assessment program has gone through several stages. During the first three years, emphasis was on the introduction of student learning outcomes assessment concepts and practices to the campus community. During this period, assessment experts were brought to campus to conduct workshops and consultation sessions with faculty and staff, mini-grants were offered to support course-related assessment projects, and a newsletter was published to familiarize the campus with assessment. During the next stage, these activities continued and the mini-grant program was expanded to include schoolwide or collegewide assessment. (For more information on the early years of assessment at SU, see Vincow, 1997a, 1997b.)

During the third stage of the assessment program, efforts were concentrated on three very practical activities intended to lay a firm foundation for a more systematic and sustained approach to assessment. The first was Campus Conversations, which were held with faculty, staff, and administrators to discuss their issues about assessment. Through these conversations, the committee also was able to identify Ongoing Efforts, which were posted on the All University Student Learning Outcomes Assessment Committee (AUSLOAC) Web site as examples of assessment practices. The third activity included pilot assessment projects that gave academic affairs and student affairs staff an opportunity to experiment with assessment and to share what they were learning with others.

Now we are at the stage of institutionalizing assessment. Two pillars support this stage: (1) the academic plan recently developed by the vice chancellor for academic affairs and provost, Debbie Freund (see Freund, 2001), and (2) the evolving expectations of external accrediting agencies, including the Middles States Commission on Higher Education, the New York State Education Department, and specialized and disciplinary accrediting associations.

Most of the strategies related to retention and assessment are subsumed under initiative 2 of the academic plan ("Ensure greater student success"). The main elements of the strategy for retention are engagement and accountability. Faculty, students, and staff across the university must become engaged in the processes of teaching and learning, both in and outside the classroom. And they must be held accountable for the successful accomplishment of student learning outcomes. In the end, this should lead to persistence of students to the completion of their degrees and successful placement. Underlying these fundamental elements of retention is the assessment of student learning.

The academic plan includes a strategy for developing and implementing an ongoing process to assess student learning under the direction of the University Assessment Council. All units in Academic Affairs and Student Affairs will submit annual progress reports on the implementation of their assessment plans to the University Assessment Council for review. Assessment plans should allow them to answer important and interesting questions, make maximum use of existing sources and methods of gathering information about student learning, and be constructed in light of the academic plan; the expectations of the Middle States Commission on Higher Education, the New York State Education Department, and relevant professional and disciplinary accrediting associations; and any assessment plans or practices already in place.

This latter element is a somewhat unique feature of assessment at Syracuse University. A thorough study has been conducted (O'Brien, 2001) in order to understand the relationship of internal, ongoing student learning outcomes assessment to periodic external accreditation reviews. This will result in a campuswide plan for assessment that uses faculty and staff resources efficiently and effectively.

The University Assessment Council (UAC) is charged with reviewing assessment plans and annual reports based on the following criteria: the extent to which faculty or staff are engaged in describing intended student learning; the clarity of the questions they ask about teaching and learning; and the actual use of information they collect to answer questions about learning and to guide subsequent changes in their educational programs, courses, and activities and in their assessment process. The UAC also will review the reports to ensure that the ongoing collective efforts of school, college, and student affairs units to assess student learning and improve educational effectiveness make sense—that is, are meaningful, manageable, and sustainable (Program Assessment Consultation Team, 1999) and satisfy requirements placed on SU by regional, state, and disciplinary accrediting bodies. In doing so, the UAC will provide oversight, coordination, and technical assistance for the university's assessment efforts.

For more information about assessment at Syracuse University contact Ron Cavanagh, Vice President for Undergraduate Studies, Syracuse
University, 304 Steele Hall, Syracuse, NY 13244, phone: 315–443–1899;
e-mail: <rrcavana@syr.edu>.

References

Freund, D. A. "A Strategic Partnership for Innovative Research and Education (A-
SPIRE): An Academic Plan for Syracuse University."
[http://acadplan.syr.edu/Acadplan418.html]. Apr. 2001.

O'Brien, J. G. Syracuse, N.Y.: Center for Support of Teaching and Learning, Syracuse
University, June 2001.

Program Assessment Consultation Team (PACT). Bakersfield: California State University, July 21, 1999.

Vincow, G. "Advancing Quality of Educational Outcomes Through Assessment: Defining Goals." Syracuse, N.Y.: Syracuse University, Feb. 1997a.

Vincow, G. "Introducing the Next Phase of Assessment at Syracuse: Address to the
Faculty." [http://www.syr.edu/acadaff/assessmt/0297sph.html]. Feb. 26, 1997b.

Ronald C. Cavanagh is vice president and associate professor for undergraduate
studies; Franklin P. Wilbur is executive director of the Center for Support of Teaching and Learning, associate vice president for undergraduate studies, and adjunct
faculty in the Department of Instructional Design, Development, and Evaluation for
the Graduate School of Education; and Peter J. Gray is associate director for the
Center for Support of Teaching and Learning. All are at Syracuse University.

The Assessment Outcomes Program at California State University, Northridge: A Model for Program Improvement

Roberta E. Madison, Norman Fullner, Paul Baum

*Here is how one state university brought assessment of student learning out-
comes to its various departments and programs. The authors describe the kind
of training and leadership required to engage administrators, faculty, and staff*

across the university—and they discuss in detail assessment in two depart-
ments, art and business administration and economics. From Assessment
Update *11:5. For a listing of hallmarks illustrated in this article see the ma-*
trix on page 8.

This article shows how the "A" word, assessment, was turned into the
"Aah!!" word at a large urban public university—California State University, Northridge (CSUN). CSUN was one of the first in a twenty-two-
campus system to develop and implement a faculty-led, administratively
supported department or program outcomes-assessment policy with a
focus on student learning.

After returning from the 1991 AAHE Assessment Conference in
Washington, D.C., the CSUN faculty and administrative participants
held a university-wide workshop to disseminate their learnings. A major
accomplishment of this session was the formation of the Assessment Din-
ner Group, composed of interested faculty and administrators who met
monthly for more than three years. This group initiated an assessment
policy that was later refined by the Educational Policy Committee and
the Senate Executive Committee. After a few iterations, the policy was
passed by the Faculty Senate and signed by the president of CSUN. The
policy specified the initial steps and objectives of the current program.

To implement the policy, the provost appointed a coordinator of assessment and the Educational Policies Committee appointed an assessment subcommittee. All departments and programs, as required by the
policy, appointed a liaison. The policy also stipulated that the university
must make grants available to departments to develop assessment plans.
Grants were awarded to sixteen departments.

Over a two-year period, two experts were invited to assist faculty and
administrators in learning about assessment techniques. The sessions were
well attended and before the second expert left more than a dozen departments had submitted their assessment plans for the expert to review.
Assessment methods included portfolios, capstone courses, senior seminars and papers, juried performances, and research projects.

The department and program liaisons began meeting monthly soon
after the policy went into effect. This venue is used to share ideas and de-

velop new methods for reporting assessment plans. Out of this group came the interim assessment form. Each department and program was to complete the form by providing the following information: four goals, four measurable objectives, procedures for measuring the objectives, and methods for sharing results with the department or program faculty.

As of this writing, 96 percent of the departments and programs (including the university library) have submitted assessment plans. A matrix that is constantly updated was designed to keep the associate vice president of academic affairs informed of the progress of program assessment. Each year the associate vice president and the assessment coordinator meet with the college deans to discuss the plans of the departments in their respective colleges and any new developments.

Assessment liaisons share the results of assessment with the department faculty. To date, more than 50 percent of the academic departments, including art, biology, business administration and economics, English, foreign languages, history, library, music, nursing, psychology, physics and astronomy, secondary education, special education, and women's studies, have completed some outcomes assessment. Following are two examples.

Example from Art

When implementing program assessment in a large university, it is important not only to recognize the varied nature of subject disciplines but also to demonstrate that each program can implement an assessment plan. Art is among those disciplines that place an emphasis on performance. Therefore, this program is often viewed as different from disciplines that emphasize the accumulation and application of knowledge. At CSUN, however, we have tried to demonstrate that programs emphasizing performance can implement valid program assessment. Art provides an example of a program that

- Is in the early stages of implementing its assessment procedures
- Is viewed as difficult to assess
- Includes qualitative assessment procedures

- Involves faculty who may not be familiar with quantitative methods used in assessment

Key components of the art program assessment plan are as follows:

1. *Art 200: Introduction to Visual Technology.* Students in this course learn about computer software programs that relate to art. They demonstrate their understanding of specific fundamentals by using these programs to answer questions that relate to the program's prerequisite introductory drawing and design courses. This assessment is designed to be limited to cognitive content. Early information from this procedure will take time to interpret because it is difficult to determine whether, or to what degree, the accumulation of this content corresponds to performance in art.

2. *Town hall meetings.* Each semester the department chair conducts one or more meetings for students only. In these meetings, students usually state their opinions or indicate their level of satisfaction on matters related to the art program. The chair reports the students' responses to outcome objectives to the department. In the report, student confidentiality is rigorously maintained.

3. *Art 438: Senior Projects.* Most of the projects in this course are used to assess art program outcome objectives. Students come to this course after concentrated coursework in one or more fields of art. Both collaboratively and as individual artist-scholars, they demonstrate their ability to function as practitioners in the discipline. Course instructors report their own qualitative responses about the relationship between student work and student achievement of learning objectives. Faculty have ascertained that students do well in meeting the program's expectations in art, but students need more help to achieve oral and writing skills.

4. *Alumni survey.* Periodic campuswide alumni surveys have provided the department with data on graduates who hold high-profile positions in art or in art-related fields. However, the department plans to initiate its own study to gain information on a broader range of alumni. The survey would be designed to yield better data on graduates who enter art-related fields.

Example from Business Administration and Economics

The assessment program in the College of Business Administration and Economics helps determine the extent to which the college is meeting its objective of graduating students who can think critically, who communicate effectively both orally and in writing, who understand and apply basic business concepts, and who possess leadership skills. Various instruments have been developed to assess these skills.

The Basic Concepts in Business Test was designed by the faculty to determine the ability of graduating seniors to retain the meaning of basic business concepts. The test emphasizes the ability to recall information rather than to apply basic concepts. The latter ability is tested using a different instrument. A pilot test was given to eighty-six graduating seniors in four sections of a capstone policy course. The exam consisted of thirty-six questions, with four questions from each functional area of business, each having five possible answers. The time allotted for the test was fifty minutes. On average, the graduating seniors recalled about half of the basic concepts. A regression analysis was conducted to explain variation in test scores. The variables used were the students' grade point averages (GPA), their majors, and the time required to complete the test. These variables collectively explained 23 percent of the variation in test scores. The only significant predictors of students' test scores were their GPAs and whether they majored in accounting. The regression coefficient for GPA revealed, for example, that if a student's GPA increased from 2.0 to 3.0, the student's test score could be expected to increase by 8.8 points. The regression coefficient for accounting indicated that an accounting major can be expected to attain a score 6.7 points higher than the scores achieved by other majors, independent of the accounting student's GPA. The lack of significance of some of the other variables could be due to the relatively small sample sizes for some of the majors.

Based on the pilot results, the test was given to four hundred students in the remaining sections of the course. Cronbach's alpha was computed to measure the reliability of the test. The overall reliability was low, indicating that the test questions measure different traits, as expected. Thus, a student could do well in, for example, marketing but not finance because different attributes are required in each of these functional areas. The reliability within each functional area was also low, indicating, for instance, that a marketing student might do well in advertising but not in marketing strategy. High reliability within and between functional areas would not be desirable, because it would imply that some test questions repeat the same information and are therefore redundant. The test appears to have high discrimination value because the scores were unrelated to major, a variable that should have no effect on the trait being measured, namely, knowledge of basic business concepts.

Other Assessment Activities

Other assessment activities in the college included an employer survey and a student satisfaction survey. The employer survey asked the college's external customers, companies that hire graduates, to rate the quality of the graduates' communication skills, computer skills, teamwork, problem solving, and critical thinking, and their understanding of basic business concepts during their first year of employment. The rating in each category ranged from 0 (unacceptable) to 4 (outstanding), with 2 being average. CSUN graduates were rated above average in each category.

The student satisfaction survey, sponsored by the college's accrediting agency, compared the level of student satisfaction with, for example, the college's teaching, facilities, advising, and career center to the levels of student satisfaction among a group of six comparable colleges. Overall, the average level of student satisfaction at CSUN exceeded the overall average level of satisfaction at the comparable colleges.

Roberta E. Madison is university outcomes assessment coordinator, Norman Fullner is professor of art, and Paul Baum is director of assessment outcomes in the College of Business Administration and Economics at California State University, Northridge.

Assessment of a Multidisciplinary Curriculum: The West Point Experience

James JF Forest, Bruce Keith

The focus of education at West Point is graduating students who can anticipate and respond effectively to the uncertainties of a changing technological, social, political, and economic world. The authors describe their approach, which involves breaking down this central objective into measurable goals. From Assessment Update 15:2. For a listing of hallmarks illustrated in this article see the matrix on page 8.

Education scholars generally agree that the most robust forms of assessment are driven by a clear set of goals and objectives and are used to manage an institution's academic program more effectively. Toward this end, accreditation agencies request demonstrable evidence in response to the seemingly simple question of how a curriculum supports students' achievement of a program's stated goals. However, the complexities inherent in the structure and context of a liberal arts curriculum often present formidable challenges to providing this evidence.

With encouragement from Trudy Banta and Peter Gray, we will illustrate West Point's efforts to meet these challenges in several consecutive issues of *Assessment Update*. We will discuss each of our academic program goals by (1) detailing the structure, process, and content of student experiences that contribute to the achievement of the goal; (2) describing what our assessment evidence is telling us about student achievement of the goal; and (3) reviewing how we use this evidence to improve the quality of the curriculum.

Institutional Context

The service academies are unique elements of the American higher education landscape. As training grounds for future officers of the nation's armed forces, each academy is dedicated to the highest standards of academic, military, and physical education. The students who attend these institutions are typically high achievers and uniquely dedicated to the principle of service. The U.S. Military Academy (USMA) at West Point received 10,884 applicant files for the class of 2006; of these, 3,819 were nominated for appointment to the academy, and 1,197 were accepted. Cadet (student) profiles of those accepted are comparable to those of many of the nation's most prominent colleges and universities.

The faculty consist of civilian and military personnel with long-term appointments as well as a large number of rotating junior military officers. The rotating faculty, representing approximately two-thirds of all faculty, are high-achieving captains selected for their ability to complete a graduate program within two years and serve as USMA instructors for an additional two or three years. They, more than any other faculty, provide cadets with the direct connection between recent military field experience and academics. All members of the faculty share the responsibility of cadet development, serving as representatives to athletic teams and intramural or academic clubs. As such, members of the staff and faculty are expected to contribute to a developmental system that places a premium on educating cadets and inspiring them to pursue careers as commissioned officers. West Point's student-centered approach to teaching and learning demands a high level of faculty collaboration, which in turn lends credibility to our collective focus on assessment as a vehicle for curricular renewal.

The Academic Program and Assessment System

Many observers are surprised to learn that the general educational experience of West Point cadets is quite comparable to that of the most highly regarded liberal arts institutions in the world. Once almost exclusively focused on civil engineering, the current West Point curriculum balances the physical sciences and engineering with the humanities and social sciences. Moreover, students experience interdisciplinary opportunities for problem solving and decision making, which we believe are essential to success as a commissioned army officer.

The diversity of tasks undertaken by the U.S. Army requires leaders whose education is grounded solidly in a common professional curriculum, one that meets the multiple challenges of military service and continuing professional development. The entire academic program is guided by a single overarching goal: to enable its graduates to anticipate and to respond effectively to the uncertainties of a changing technological, social, political, and economic world. From this goal, the U.S. Military Academy derives a set of ten specific academic program goals that address army needs and reflect the attributes that the academy seeks to develop in its graduates. Specifically, on achieving the overarching academic program goal, graduates will be able to (1) think and act creatively, (2) recognize moral issues and apply ethical considerations in decision making, (3) communicate effectively, and (4) demonstrate the capability and desire to pursue progressive and continued intellectual development. Moreover, graduates will demonstrate proficiency in six domains of knowledge: (5) engineering and technology, (6) mathematics and science, (7) information technology, (8) historical perspective, (9) cultural perspective, and (10) understanding human behavior. The rationale and amplification of these goals are illustrated in an operational concept document, *Educating Future Army Officers in a Changing World*, which has been written collaboratively by and for the USMA faculty.

While many colleges and universities have general educational goals similar to those of the U.S. Military Academy, West Point's mission of educating cadets for career service as professional army officers adds a unique contextual dimension. Goal achievement is primarily structured around thirty core courses. Within each of these required courses, the faculty collaboratively design a common course syllabus and learning materials to ensure that each cadet receives a comparable academic experience. Faculty also play an important role in assessing cadets' outcomes through a collaborative structure of teams and committees. Each of the academic program goals was developed and is regularly monitored by a goal team, comprising between six and fifteen military and civilian members of the faculty. The chairs of each goal team form the Assessment Steering Committee, which coordinates the goals and assessment system at the program level.

The faculty goal teams meet regularly to review the assessment data gathered through cadet surveys of freshmen and seniors, graduates, and commanders, as well as focus group data collected from battalion commanders. In addition to these indirect, typically summative, measures, goal teams also analyze course-embedded indicators—course products such as research papers, final exams, and capstone projects—that represent direct, formative measures of student goal achievement. The regular collection of these complementary forms of data has, over the past seven years, allowed the U.S. Military Academy to develop a robust longitudinal assessment database through which we analyze students' progressive achievement of the academic program goals as well as draw comparisons among successive cohorts.

In the next issue of *Assessment Update*, we will focus on our "understanding human behavior" goal and describe in greater detail our assessment activities in this area—including rubric design and embedded curricular indicators—which contribute to our understanding of student outcomes and the effective management of our academic program.

James JF Forest is assistant professor of political science and assistant dean for academic assessment and Bruce Keith is professor of sociology and associate dean for academic affairs at the United States Military Academy, West Point, New York.

Assessment at the University of Scranton

Peter J. Gray

Here is a comprehensive assessment program that, drawing on input from faculty, staff, and students, assesses academic outcomes in both general education and the major, as well as such broad individual outcomes as character and leadership. A particularly effective method of encouraging academic units to collect and use assessment data is the provost's request for an annual report from de-

partment chairs which includes evidence that desired student outcomes are being achieved. From Assessment Update *11:4. For a listing of hallmarks illustrated in this article see the matrix on page 8.*

Interest in assessment at the University of Scranton began with the 1987–88 accreditation self-study, "in which 'outcomes' or 'assessment' was one of the special topics selected for study" (Assessment and Institutional Research Office, 1996b, p. 6). Following the successful accreditation effort, a grant was received from the Council for the Advancement of Private Higher Education. The grant provided resources that led to the development of an evaluation plan for the university's revised general education curriculum, the initiation of departmental evaluation of majors, the creation of assessment plans related to student development outcomes, affiliation with the Higher Education Data Sharing Consortium, and the development of an assessment plan for the university's strategic plan. Subsequently, a university-wide assessment committee composed of faculty, staff, and students was formed, with support to be provided by the renamed Assessment and Institutional Research Office (AIRO).

In 1996 the university's assessment plan was revised to reflect recent progress in assessment. A key feature of the plan is the guidelines for development of the University of Scranton assessment program. Briefly, these guidelines state that the principal focus of assessment includes students' academic and nonacademic outcomes. "Academic outcomes center mainly on the knowledge and skills developed in the major field of study and on the intended outcomes of general education. Non-academic outcomes include such matters as the development of character, moral sensibilities, proclivities towards leadership and volunteer work, etc." (Assessment and Institutional Research Office, 1996b, p. 2). Determination of the student outcomes that should be addressed is informed by the university's mission statement. The assessment plan attempts to stimulate the development of assessment activities by individual academic and nonacademic units that are modest in scope and that produce information for purposes of improvement. Further, the results of assessment activities should be communicated to the university community.

Responsibility for implementation of the assessment plan rests with the AIRO, with the university-wide assessment committee, and with local unit chairs and directors. Responsibility for development and implementation of the plan has been assigned to AIRO, which reports to the provost–academic vice president. The faculty, staff, students, and alumni on the assessment committee help to define and provide ongoing direction for assessment. More specifically, the committee helps to identify the key assessment indicators, provides advice on assessment processes, contributes to assessment reports, and interprets the meaning of the national assessment movement for the university. Individual units are involved in assessment through responsibility for developing annual reports, involvement in program reviews, and updating strategic plans. Chairs, directors, faculty, and staff may be engaged in these assessment activities at the unit level.

Three major components constitute the University of Scranton's assessment plan: university-wide sources of information, unit-level assessment processes, and periodic studies of selected issues.

University-Wide Sources of Information

Sources of information about all or nearly all students involve data collected directly from students through surveys. A senior survey gathers information about students' reflections on their college experience at the time of their graduation. (See, for example, Assessment and Institutional Research Office, 1994.) Other surveys focus on students' postgraduation placement, their comments about their current activities, and their evaluation of their educational experience three to five years after graduation. (See, for example, Assessment and Institutional Research Office, 1998a, 1998b, 1998c, and 1999.) Supplementary questions added to standard surveys often explore student and alumni reactions to unique aspects of the university's mission as a Jesuit institution. Other sources of information include data on student retention and graduation rates. Information gained from all of these sources is reported to the entire campus community. This information has formed the basis for discussions of general university improvements in such areas as enrollment management and career services.

One area of assessment that has not yet been fully developed is assessment of the general education program. Two directions are anticipated. The first is to embed assessment procedures in the courses of the revised general education program. The second is to identify sources of information about the outcomes of general education beyond those available from course-embedded assessments or from self-reports of progress in senior and alumni surveys.

Unit-Level Assessment Processes

Specific improvements in academic and nonacademic programs result from the implementation of unit-level assessment processes. Unit-level processes are the second component of the University of Scranton assessment plan. In their article in the September-October 1997 issue of *Assessment Update*, Hogan and Stamford wrote about strategies they have used to encourage departments to engage in assessment activities. They acknowledge that there is a gap between the principle that faculty play an especially important role in assessing student learning and the fact that there is a lack of faculty involvement in assessment activities. They also point out that "one way to encourage faculty involvement is through the academic department structure" because "the department is often the key change agent for any type of reform. . . . Adopting assessment strategies and, more important, ensuring that assessment information is utilized effectively can depend heavily on department involvement" (p. 4). At the University of Scranton the department annual report has been used as one mechanism for encouraging assessment at the department level.

The provost requests from each department an annual report that looks forward to the next year and is based on reflection on the accomplishments of the previous year. These reports chart the progress of new programs, support requests for faculty and staff positions, identify capital improvements needed, and so on. The following language has been inserted in the provost's request: "Identify any student outcomes information which the department has collected and/or discussed during the past year. Such information might include follow-up of graduates, surveys of students, graduates' test scores, and similar types of information" (Hogan and Stamford, 1997, p. 4). It should be noted that departments were not *required* to do anything in particular other than report what they had done. Over a three-year period the extent of compliance with this request went from about 50 percent to more than 90 percent, just through the process of reporting back to department chairs brief summaries of what had been reported by the departments, without naming them.

As a follow-up to the request for reports, luncheon meetings are held with small groups of department chairs to address two issues: what the chairs are trying to accomplish with their students and any evidence they have that they are successful. These meetings occur twice in the fall and twice in the spring. After several rounds of meetings, the chairs have learned about such department-level assessment activities as student surveys, standardized tests, focus groups, and exit interviews.

In addition to annual reports, a periodic program review process is in place at the University of Scranton that occurs approximately every seven years for a given department. Program reviews may coincide with external accreditation reviews. There are similar procedures for program review for both academic departments and units in the student affairs division. The ultimate purpose of the program review process, as with assessment in general, is improvement. "Development of specific, practical suggestions for the next several years is of special interest" (Assessment and Institutional Research Office, 1996a, p. 1). Program reviews are intended primarily for the faculty members responsible for a program and the academic administrators who oversee it, although the reports are available to other campus groups. The major categories for review include the purpose and objectives of the program and its curriculum, students, and faculty. In addition, a unit's facilities and support services are considered, as are its finances and productivity. Finally, the future directions and objectives of the program are included in the program review.

The program review guidelines include descriptions of each of these categories as well as relevant sources of information. For example, "Useful documents for statements about the purposes or objectives of the program include the catalog, recruitment materials, departmental annual reports, and college or university mission statements" (Assessment and

Institutional Research Office, 1996a, p. 5). Various reports produced by the AIRO are cited as relevant sources of information about students. However, departments are directed to supplement these sources with any other information gathered locally, especially information about the extent to which students are achieving the departments' identified objectives.

Periodic Studies of Selected Issues

The third component of the University of Scranton assessment plan is periodic studies of selected issues. A series of reports produced by the Student Affairs Division, called *Findings to Action*, contains descriptions of some of the assessment findings related to studies in this area. Sources of these findings include a survey of commuting students, a freshman survey, and a quality-of-student-life survey. These surveys cover such topics as how much time commuters spend on campus outside class, where they spend their time, and what inhibits them from getting more involved in campus life. In addition, freshman students' academic aspirations, self-confidence, financial concerns, and signs of academic disengagement were studied. Further, student satisfaction with the quality of residential programs, the room selection process, and the visitation and alcohol policies were assessed as part of the quality-of-student-life survey.

Another example of a periodic study is the university's participation in the Higher Education Research Institute's faculty survey, first in 1992, then in 1996, and again in 1999. The findings of these surveys include information about faculty members' goals regarding scholarship, service, and teaching.

A Dynamic and Evolving Process

In the future, improvements will be sought in methods for assessing the outcomes of the general education program, methods for the distribution and use of assessment information, involvement of academic departments in devising their own assessment strategies, alumni follow-up, understanding students' undergraduate careers from entry to graduation, and the articulation of assessment and the university's mission. Clearly, assessment at the University of Scranton is a dynamic and evolving process.

For more information, please contact Thomas P. Hogan, director of assessment and the Institutional Research Office, University of Scranton, Scranton, PA 18510–4629 (717–941–6344).

References

Assessment and Institutional Research Office. *Freshman to Senior Changes for the Class of 1993: A Supplement to the Senior Survey Report for the University of Scranton.* Scranton, Pa.: University of Scranton, Apr. 1994.

Assessment and Institutional Research Office. *The Academic Program Review at the University of Scranton.* Scranton, Pa.: University of Scranton, Jan. 1996a.

Assessment and Institutional Research Office. *The University of Scranton Assessment Plan.* Scranton, Pa.: University of Scranton, Oct. 1996b.

Assessment and Institutional Research Office. *1997 Alumni Survey: Class of 1991 Reports. Report 1: Who Are They?* Scranton, Pa.: University of Scranton, Mar. 1998a.

Assessment and Institutional Research Office. *1997 Alumni Survey: Class of 1991 Reports. Report 2: What Are They Doing?* Scranton, Pa.: University of Scranton, Mar. 1998b.

Assessment and Institutional Research Office. *1997 Alumni Survey: Class of 1991 Reports. Report 4: Special Jesuit Mission and Comments.* Scranton, Pa.: University of Scranton, May 1998c.

Assessment and Institutional Research Office. *1997 Alumni Survey: Class of 1991 Reports. Report 3: Evaluation of Their Undergraduate Education.* Scranton, Pa.: University of Scranton, Mar. 1999.

Higher Education Research Institute (1992–1993). National Norms for 1992–1993 HERI Faculty Survey Report. Los Angeles: University of California, Los Angeles.

Higher Education Research Institute (1995–1996). National Norms for 1995–1996 HERI Faculty Survey Report. Los Angeles: University of California, Los Angeles.

Hogan, T. P., and Stamford, A. M. "Encouraging Departments to Engage in Assessment Activities." *Assessment Update*, 1997, 9(5), 4–5, 14.

Peter J. Gray is associate director of the Center for Support of Teaching and Learning, Syracuse University.

Specific Strategies for Advancing the Hallmarks

That Second Look at Student Work: A Strategy for Engaging Faculty in Outcomes Assessment

Trudy W. Banta

Faculty use assessment of individual student work regularly to assign grades. But, as Trudy Banta argues, in order to understand whether courses, methods, and curricula are effective requires that they take a second look at student work to see where group strengths and weaknesses may lie. Here Banta describes what that involves. From Assessment Update 12:1. For a listing of hallmarks illustrated in this article see the matrix on page 8.

In the last five weeks I have visited with faculty on campuses in Connecticut, Missouri, Utah, and West Virginia, as well as my own. The substance of many of these recent conversations has convinced me to take another long look at the process of engaging faculty in outcomes assessment. This is a developmental process, with several steps that must be considered and worked through. There is nothing sacred about the order in which these activities occur, but a successful process will include all of them.

Most faculty say, "Yes," when asked if they assess student learning. "We ask students to write papers and do projects; we evaluate these and give tests; and we assign grades. Isn't that enough?" Those of us who serve as assessment advocates respond that all of the methods used to evaluate the work of individual students *may* be helpful in what we now call outcomes assessment—that is, measuring the effectiveness of courses and curricula in promoting student learning. But in this more comprehensive sense of assessing outcomes, a second look at student work is needed. That is, if we seek to demonstrate course and program effectiveness, we must look at student work not just individually but also collectively—across students in a course, across sections of the same course, and across courses in a disciplinary major—to see where learning is at a satisfactory level for most, what needs to be retaught or taught in a different way for some, and which approaches to teaching produce the most learning for which students. Only by taking that second look can we tell what is working in our classrooms and what may need to be changed.

Most faculty are interested in finding out what helps students learn. They don't want to spend a semester teaching concepts that turn out to be grasped fully by less than half the class, misunderstood by some, and retained beyond the date of the final exam by only a few. Moreover, if a new approach to teaching (such as Web-based modules, problem-based learning, case studies, or group projects) is attempted, most faculty would like to know if the new method works better than the methods formerly used. Appealing to faculty curiosity about what works and drawing on their dedication to helping students learn—and to improving student learning continuously—are the most compelling of all approaches to engaging faculty in outcomes assessment. But there are others, such as mandates for assessment from the provost, board of trustees, or state legislature, or the obligation to satisfy an accrediting agency.

If faculty can be convinced through intrinsic or extrinsic motivation that outcomes assessment is worth their own second look, an important first barrier to engagement has been hurdled, and the next step in the process of involvement can begin.

We suggest that effective outcomes assessment has its foundation in explicit goals for student learning. (Some faculty begin by collecting some data first, but they are soon confronted with the need for a statement of desired outcomes to provide a context for understanding the data.) And while each faculty member must have goals for learning in each of his or her courses, assessment in the disciplinary major requires agreement among faculty in the discipline on a statement of what students should know and be able to do when they complete their programs of study in the major.

Most faculty have written their course objectives—if they have written them at all—in terms of what they will teach or what topics they will cover rather than in terms of what students will learn. And most have not even considered collaborating with colleagues to develop a collective, comprehensive statement of expectations for student learning in the major.

Developing goals for student learning in the major can proceed in any of several ways. The faculty as a whole may sit down with a blank page and construct a first draft of desired knowledge and skills on the basis of group discussion. Alternatively, each faculty member can contribute a list of learning outcomes for each course he or she teaches, and the first draft of departmental outcomes can be based on a composite of the outcomes specified for all courses. Barbara Walvoord (personal communication, 1999) has suggested that faculty begin by reviewing the assignments and tests they give, then identifying the knowledge and skills they ask students to practice in assignments and master for tests. This is a third way to approach the development of a first draft of desired outcomes for a major. Obviously, revising the initial draft is an indispensable next step. Reaching consensus on learning outcomes is crucial to successful assessment and may take months or years to achieve.

A next step is to ascertain where and how students will learn the knowledge and skills characterized as essential for a major in the discipline. Will students learn and practice a skill in a course, in an internship, or in some other out-of-class setting? If this link is not made explicitly, some students may finish all their coursework without having had the opportunity to develop some critical skill.

Then faculty might ask, "What evidence that students have learned the desired knowledge and skills will we consider credible?" Sometimes there is a standardized test or questionnaire that faculty agree will measure some of the specified learning. A useful standardized instrument will yield subscale scores and item scores that faculty can use to assess specific student strengths and weaknesses. But most often no standardized instruments are available in the discipline, or those that are available do not provide coverage of all knowledge and skills faculty consider important. Thus we encourage faculty to use assignments, their own quizzes and exams, papers and projects, fieldwork evaluations, portfolios—all the measures they would employ in assigning grades to individual students—as outcomes assessment measures.

Faculty are fully prepared to take that second look at students' scores on standardized instruments. They select an instrument because it provides subscale and perhaps even item scores. They inspect those scores for evidence of student strengths and weaknesses. But faculty are not fully prepared to take that second look at student performance on locally developed instruments. There is a need to go back to the matrix specifying (1) desired knowledge and skills in the major, (2) sites for learning the knowledge and skills, and (3) methods of assessing student mastery of the knowledge and skills. If a given skill is to be assessed via a project and a series of test questions in one or more courses, a group of faculty must assemble those artifacts, which have been assessed once by a course instructor for the purpose of giving feedback and grades to individual students, and give them a second review to see how many students have mastered the skill. If the disciplinary faculty have agreed that at least 80 percent of the program graduates should have mastered the skill, and only 65 percent are found to have done so, then presumably something needs to change. The students need more and perhaps different ways to practice the skill in the curriculum.

If faculty can be convinced to take a second look at the evidence of student learning—both in- and out-of-class—that they themselves have constructed, the next steps in assessment should follow more easily. Faculty must consider collectively the findings derived from assessment, then actually use the findings to improve courses, curricula, and student support services such as advising and tutoring. There may be resistance to changing time-honored approaches, particularly if outcomes assessment provides the first hint that an approach is not working as expected. In these cases, two or three sets of findings that corroborate each other may be needed to convince faculty that changes really are needed.

Collaborating on statements of learning outcomes for the major, writing outcomes using action verbs that suggest methods of assessment, linking learning outcomes to opportunities for learning in courses and outside class, developing sources of credible evidence of student learning, studying those standardized or locally developed sources for clues about what is working well in promoting student learning and what may need to be changed, collectively considering the findings to ascertain their implications, and making use of findings to initiate warranted improvements—these are the steps that ultimately must be undertaken in a complete and successful outcomes assessment initiative. Each of these steps takes time, and faculty need support for doing things that many have never done before.

For campuswide outcomes assessment to succeed, the president or the provost or both must say it is important and provide essential support mechanisms. These include opportunities for faculty and student affairs professionals to attend regional and national assessment conferences together; on-campus seminars on aspects of assessment, perhaps led by an external consultant from time to time; a campuswide assessment committee with broad representation; one or more offices charged with coordinating data-gathering initiatives such as surveys and standardized tests; incorporation of outcomes assessment in the scholarship of teaching in promotion and tenure guidelines; and release time for faculty who assume major roles in the outcomes assessment initiative. Faculty development is crucial: faculty groups can begin by reading relevant literature on assessment; then they may need to develop workshops on writing objectives or using assessment methods such as portfolios. As soon as units have findings to share, seminars or best-practice fairs should be held. Grants for exploratory work such as instrument development have been very helpful on some campuses.

For many faculty outcomes assessment is just one more important development on which they are asked to spend time. Fortunately, time spent now to design assessment initiatives that will demonstrate the relative effectiveness of various approaches to educating students promises future time savings in evaluating student work and in cutting short explorations of blind alleys.

Lessons Learned in the Assessment School of Hard Knocks: Guidelines and Strategies to Encourage Faculty Ownership and Involvement in Outcomes Assessment

Carolyn J. Haessig, Armand S. La Potin

Faculty involvement in assessment is critical, but it is often hard to achieve. As the authors point out, getting faculty engaged in assessment is a matter of understanding faculty concerns, finding ways to address these concerns, and taking the time to educate faculty about the purpose, methods, and value of assessment. Here are specific guidelines for doing just that. From Assessment Update 11:5. For a listing of hallmarks illustrated in this article see the matrix on page 8.

We chaired our college's Outcomes Assessment Task Force, which included faculty and support staff selected to represent academic affairs, student development, and finance and administration. The task force was charged with planning and coordinating campuswide efforts to articulate and assess student outcomes in academic and student development programs.

The college's initial concern was to address the accreditation guidelines mandated by the Middle States Association (MSA), its regional accrediting body, for the college's five-year periodic review in 1998.

Nevertheless, the MSA expects assessment to be ongoing, and college officials recognize the need for it. Consequently, the Outcomes Assessment Task Force is mandated (some might say challenged!) to lead staff and faculty in particular in embracing and conducting assessment.

We organized and were the primary conductors of a series of hearings and workshops for faculty and staff. Following are some general guidelines and strategies drawn from our experience.

Convey a sense of urgency about the need to conduct assessment. Faculty may need to be convinced that they can neither avoid nor delay articulating and assessing student learning. Although the reasons may vary among institutions, some common ones for undertaking assessment *immediately* include the mandates of accrediting agencies or governing bodies, the demands of other external stakeholders, and a college's need to ascertain and demonstrate that limited instructional resources are being effectively and efficiently deployed.

Strategies for creating a sense of urgency with regard to assessment include preparing an action plan and a time line so that faculty and staff have a clear understanding of when the task needs to be started, what must be accomplished, and who must accomplish it.

It is important to stress at the outset that there is urgency about getting started and that assessment will be ongoing. Although there are deadlines that must be met, there is no point at which assessment of student learning is finished.

Anticipate and address faculty concerns early in the process. Faculty can be expected to resist change and present reasons why student learning outcomes cannot be articulated or assessed. For example, typical reactions to assessment include the following:

- *"I can't."* The arguments against starting or continuing assessment activities can be expected to include lack of time, personnel, or support resources.
- *"I won't."* Some view assessment as intrusive or professionally demeaning. Some may even see it as a plot to erode their academic freedom.

- *"I shouldn't have to."* Some believe (or hope) that assessment is an administrative rather than a faculty activity.
- *"I've already done that."* Some insist that they already assess student learning through their course grading processes, even though they have not or cannot explain the expectations that resulted in awarding a given grade. Others believe that assessment is the evaluation of their departments and academic programs conducted with the implicit objective of justifying existing or future resources. Note that although it is important to recognize faculty sensitivities, it is essential to avoid getting bogged down in philosophical discussions.

Some faculty concerns can be addressed by being clear about who will see the results and what will be done with the information submitted. It is useful as well to explain at the outset how faculty can benefit directly and individually from the process and the outcomes. For example, sharing expected outcomes with students has helped to motivate students, which can provide faculty with more dynamic classroom experiences.

Provide opportunities to enhance faculty ownership in the assessment process as early as possible. For most colleges, the first step in the assessment process is to formulate an institutional assessment plan. Faculty can and must be involved in the development and refinement of this plan. They should have several opportunities to affect the plan while it is being formulated and adopted. Faculty must serve on the group charged with formulating the plan. All faculty should be invited to open hearings in which the plan is reviewed for comments and suggestions.

Provide knowledge of how to conduct assessment. Faculty may have varying degrees of understanding and experience with each of the components of assessment: connecting programmatic goals to the college mission, articulating measurable student outcomes, identifying relevant experiences to achieve outcomes, identifying and applying techniques to measure achievement of outcomes, summarizing and reporting results, and using results to improve curriculum and learning experiences. Faculty will need varied opportunities to learn how to do what is expected of them with regard to assessment. Leaders can assist by presenting workshops to demonstrate what is required and how it might be accomplished. Faculty can benefit from seeing how easy the process can be and how extensively it is used by their colleagues on other campuses. Techniques and examples should be simple to use, broadly applicable, and cost-effective. Faculty may benefit from exploring any of the numerous institutional Web sites that include assessment plans, techniques, and outcomes.

Remember that institutional support is critical to faculty commitment. Faculty must feel that their college president, provost, and academic deans wholeheartedly endorse and support the assessment process.

Administrative personnel should be prepared to send interested and strategically placed faculty to assessment workshops and conferences. The faculty sent should be those who are or will become enthusiastic supporters and willing assessment instructors.

Administrative personnel should also be willing to fund the acquisition of needed reference materials. These materials should be made readily available to faculty and their availability should be publicized.

It is important for administrators and faculty leaders to attach value to assessment and to provide appropriate recognition for those who undertake it successfully. Doing so conveys the institution's commitment to assessment.

If institutional assessment is to yield meaningful results and be ongoing, faculty leadership is critical. Faculty must be the central players in academic assessment and, where possible, assume leadership roles as well. If assessment is to succeed, faculty involvement and leadership must be incorporated into the institution's culture. This can be accomplished by helping faculty see the tangible benefits of assessment, such as how the articulation of meaningful assessment outcomes can intellectually challenge students and how articulated student outcomes can be used to enhance recruitment initiatives. Our first year was spent helping faculty to articulate student outcomes and get their feet wet in the "ocean of assessment." This year's challenge is to work with our colleagues on a micro level, to show them what assessment instruments can best be utilized to measure their student outcomes and how to make use of their data in testing these outcomes.

Carolyn J. Haessig is professor of nutrition and dietetics, and Armand S. La Potin is professor of history at SUNY-Oneonta.

Enlisting Student Aid in Assessing Department Objectives

Daniel Nelson, Kari J. Nelson

One of the many approaches to take in assessing how well the curriculum is helping students meet educational objectives is to ask students directly. What would such an approach look like? What kinds of questions will yield the most reliable and helpful responses? The authors outline in detail how they implemented such an approach. From Assessment Update 13:6. For a listing of hallmarks illustrated in this article see the matrix on page 8.

A worthy step in the early stages of assessment has been to articulate specific educational goals or objectives for the academic curriculum. Three years ago, the Psychology Department at North Central University set up 28 specific objectives that were intended to be met by participating in the department's curriculum. Believing it was time to revisit these objectives and note student progress toward their achievement, we decided to enlist the aid of students. We were interested in addressing four questions: How important do students consider the objectives developed by faculty? Where in the curriculum is each objective being met? To what degree is each objective being met across the curriculum? What do the answers to these questions tell us about the need for changes in the status of curricular objectives?

Assessment Tools

In an attempt to address these issues, two questionnaires were devised and randomly distributed to two groups of 40 students majoring in psychology. We obtained an 80 percent response rate to the first questionnaire (32 students), and a 65 percent response rate to the second (26 students). The first questionnaire simply listed each of the 28 identified curricular objectives and asked students to rate each on a scale from 0 ("not at all important to me") to 4 ("of great importance to me"). The second questionnaire used a grid format in which the first column listed curricular objectives and the first row listed each of the courses taught by the department. The boxes of the grid allowed students to rate the degree to which each objective was met in each course. Student responses ranged from 0 ("this objective was not met to any degree in this course") to 4 ("this objective was met to a very great degree in this course").

Interpreting Student Responses

The responses of students were addressed in four ways. First, means were calculated for the importance ratings of each of the objectives in the first questionnaire. Each score represented the average level of importance that students attached to the curricular objective. Objectives considered most important related to developing realistic means to achieve career and educational goals in the field of psychology. Students rated as less important objectives that were more content-oriented, such as knowledge of historical issues in the field, psychological measurement, biological bases of behavior, and so on. Overall, 23 of the 28 objectives had mean ratings of at least 3.00 ("important to me"). This indicates that these psychology students generally identify with the goals sought by the department and view all as at least somewhat important. This suggests general agreement between what the department intends and what these students desire.

In the second questionnaire, the course-by-objective grid, each objective was rated for every course. Averaging scores across each row gave mean scores for a particular objective across the curriculum. In this way, we could see the degree to which students believed each objective was being addressed across the courses taught by the department. Twenty-three of the 28 objectives had mean ratings of greater than 2.00, meaning that the bulk of the department's objectives were being met to a moderate to great degree when averaged across the curriculum. This was interpreted positively, since the courses appear to be implemented in a way that meets the department's objectives. Some of the objectives students saw as being met least successfully across the curriculum included developing clear and practical career goals, and understanding and making plans regarding graduate education.

A third way of using student responses to these questionnaires was to look at the degree to which each course met the designated curricular objectives. By averaging down each column on the second questionnaire, we could see that 17 of the 22 courses taught met the curricular objectives at an average of 2.00 ("to a moderate degree") or greater. This was interpreted positively, since the bulk of the courses met all of the objectives to at least a moderate degree. Those courses that did not meet this cutoff included a general psychology course, as well as a few of the more content-focused courses (such as Physiological Psychology). We hypothesized that the introductory freshman-level course did not meet the department's curricular objectives to a great degree because it is designed for other purposes and for students in any major. The more content-focused courses, although they were not rated highly across all of the objectives, were given high ratings in the objective areas that were specifically tied to those courses. For example, no course scored higher than Physiological Psychology on an objective dealing with understanding the biological bases of behavior.

A final way of using student responses to these questionnaires was to look at the differences between the questionnaires. Difference scores were calculated between the importance rating of each objective (from the first questionnaire) and the degree to which that objective was met across the curriculum (from the second questionnaire). Three of the objectives with the greatest differences were developing clear, practical career goals; developing realistic means for achieving these goals; and understanding and making plans regarding graduate education.

Addressing Student Responses

We perceived that a clear trend was emerging. Although a sophomore-level course called Career Seminar already had been implemented to deal with the issues of developing career and educational goals in psychology, students' responses indicated that this area needs further development. The department is considering upgrading the course from two to three semester credits, as well as spending more time concretely discussing career planning. Responses from department graduates over the past ten years may be helpful in giving students planning options as well as providing realistic time lines for career advancement. More time can be spent discussing the process of preparing for graduate school, types of graduate programs available, steps for admission, and so on. Because this course is usually taught to sophomores, we revisit these career and educational plans during the capstone course, Senior Project. At this point just prior to their departure from the institution, we think it is wise for students to revisit these career and educational options, and revise their plans if necessary. Although the culmination of the Senior Project course is a written scholarly paper, other assignments could include a written response to their reevaluation of the career and educational plans they outlined in their sophomore year. Soon-to-graduate seniors also may appreciate and benefit more than sophomores from concretizing a ten-year educational and occupational plan in a written format. We have found that seniors have questions that are much more applied and practical than those of sophomores.

Although this indirect method is not the only way to address the achievement of curricular objectives, it clearly can be helpful to ask for students' perceptions of the degree to which the intended goals of the department are being met. Another way to gather such data would be to interview recent graduates or the employers of recent graduates. Nevertheless, even with the limitations of this approach, greater understanding can be gained by enlisting students to provide their perspectives on the department's efforts.

Daniel Nelson is assessment coordinator and Kari J. Nelson is associate professor of psychology at North Central University in Minneapolis, Minnesota.

Using Student Satisfaction Assessment Data to Influence Institutional Planning

Stephanie Juillerat, Laurie A. Schreiner

The Student Satisfaction Inventory is a questionnaire that asks students how important they consider various aspects of college as well as how satisfied they are with each. The authors offer specific guidelines for arriving at accurate and meaningful interpretations of the data from this instrument and for determining what kinds of changes to make in response to the findings. From Assessment Update 11:2. For a listing of hallmarks illustrated in this article see the matrix on page 8.

One of the most important decisions an institution will make is how it will collect information about students' levels of satisfaction. Although there are several ways to assess student satisfaction, many instruments lack some critical feature, resulting in incomplete or inaccurate data (see Juillerat, 1995). The Student Satisfaction Inventory (SSI) (Schreiner and Juillerat, 1993) is a comprehensive measure that utilizes a two-dimensional approach to the assessment of student satisfaction. Each of the seventy-nine items is stated as an expectation that a student may have about some aspect of the college; students are asked to rate how important each expectation is to them (which generates an *importance score*), as well as how satisfied they are that the expectation is currently being met (which generates a *satisfaction score*). A difference score, called the *performance gap score*, is also calculated by subtracting the satisfaction score from the importance score, thus giving an indication of how well the college is meeting a particular expectation. This approach allows institutions to gather data about the level of student expectations as well as about levels of satisfaction that their expectations are being met. "By utilizing all the scores produced by the SSI, an institution can get a more comprehensive and meaningful picture of the students' assessment of the institution, as well as a plan to accurately prioritize areas for intervention" (Juillerat and Schreiner, 1996, p. 8).

The data from the SSI scores can be interpreted and utilized in a number of ways. By collecting information from students that asks not only how satisfied they are with aspects of the campus but also how important those aspects are, a college can prioritize its interventions. One way that campuses can begin to interpret their data is by developing a two-dimensional quadrant with satisfaction scores along a horizontal axis and importance scores along a vertical axis and using the median importance and satisfaction scores as the intersection point of the two axes (see Figure 1). By plotting each SSI item's coordinates on the quadrant, a system of prioritization for intervention is provided. For example, items above the median importance score and below the median satisfaction score (upper left quadrant) represent the areas in need of immediate intervention (areas that are high in importance to students but with which they are not satisfied). Items that appear in the upper right quadrant (items that are above the median importance and satisfaction scores) illuminate an institution's strengths, and items in the lower right quadrant represent areas of lesser priority. Items in the lower right quadrant may be ones in

Figure 1. Quadrant Approach to Analyzing SSI Satisfaction Data
Hypothetical Data: Safety and Security Scale

Very Important

Immediate Intervention: *High-Priority Items*	*Strengths to Be Marketed*
The campus is safe and secure for all students.	Parking lots are well-lighted and secure.

Median │ Scores

Not at All Satisfied: *Needs Intervention Soon*	*Very Satisfied* *Low-Priority Items; Possible Fund for Reallocation*
The amount of student parking space on campus is adequate.	Security staff respond quickly in emergencies.

Not at All Important

which the budget could be adjusted because, although the campus is doing very well in those areas, they are of little importance to students. This type of data analysis allows an institution to begin a system of prioritization for effective intervention.

Before a college begins to implement changes, however, a critically important first step is to clarify the prioritized data with student focus groups. Focus groups enable students to expand on the data and clarify the results before an institution begins to implement changes. Any standardized instrument is limited in its attempt to assess unique individual campuses, because not every campus uses the same terminology (for example, not every campus has a "business office") and because each campus has its own unique systems (for instance, advising systems differ from campus to campus). Therefore, it is important to talk to students and find out what they meant when they answered the questions or rated campus items. The SSI data furnish a springboard for further campus discussions—that is, they are preliminary data that can be used to guide those discussions.

Using Satisfaction Data to Effect Positive Change

Once the satisfaction data have been interpreted and prioritized, they may be used to effect change. Yet this is precisely where many campuses falter. Too many of us analyze and interpret data and make written recommendations, then watch as our data and recommendations sit on a shelf. For data to have any impact, they must be *used* effectively. There are many ways to use satisfaction data to make a positive impact on your campus.

Market your strengths. Your own campus community, as well as the outside community, donors, and prospective students, needs to hear about what you are doing well. While you are prioritizing areas for intervention, do not forget to publicize and celebrate the things you are doing right.

Address student expectations. One of the most positive features of the SSI is that it provides two dimensions to address. Sometimes students are dissatisfied because the quality of a service is genuinely poor. But students may also be dissatisfied because their expectations are not realistic. In some instances, they have unrealistically high expectations of what college is supposed to be like; in other instances their expectations are too low because no one has told them what they have a right to expect of their college. Institutions can address student expectations in a number of ways, such as by linking more effectively with students still in high school to communicate appropriate expectations, by working with admissions counselors to help them communicate realistic expectations, by providing summer bridge experiences for the underprepared, and by focusing on expectations during orientation or in a freshman seminar course.

Work on high-priority items. This is an obvious first step in the intervention process. Target those areas in which importance scores are high and satisfaction scores are low, resulting in large gap scores. These are the areas in greatest need of intervention and that will have the most leverage in changing student perceptions. Some campuses have simply focused on the lowest satisfaction scores and, for example, built multimillion-dollar parking garages in response, only to find that it had absolutely no impact on overall student satisfaction with the institution. But if students rate parking as highly important, then that is the area to target. Satisfaction scores cannot be examined in a vacuum; they must always be evaluated in light of the importance scores.

Look for interventions that are low cost, quick fix, or both. Once you have identified the high-priority items, locate ones that can be quickly remedied or that will not cost a lot of money and address them quickly. Then publicize to your students that you responded to their requests and made these changes. On one campus, several changes were made in response to the SSI results, but no one told the students that the changes were in response to their requests, and many of them did not even notice. Once the changes were pointed out (along with the reasons for them), student perceptions improved as well.

Look for items that can be fixed with information. While you are prioritizing areas for intervention, note the low satisfaction scores that seem to be a result of misperceptions. For instance, one campus does not charge a student activity fee, yet student activity fees had a very low satisfaction score and a high importance rating. The institution responded by publishing an article in the student newspaper about not charging student fees, but they went on to explain to students where their money was going. Another institution sent out a newsletter to students over the summer to update them on the changes that were being made while they were gone and to correct some misinformation floating around about the newly built residence hall.

Use SSI data for reallocating existing funds. Another way to improve institutional efficiency is to look for items with low importance scores and very high satisfaction scores and make some budget adjustments. For instance, one institution budgets a sizeable sum for the student handbook each year and has a staff member spend a considerable amount of time updating it and improving the layout and graphics. They noticed, however, that the item about the student handbook had one of the lower importance scores and one of the highest satisfaction scores—it even had a negative gap score. So instead of spending a lot of money on changing the layout and graphics, they reallocated some of the money earmarked for the handbook to another area in need. They still updated the handbook, but the staff member's time and the extra money for graphics and layout were spent elsewhere.

Create quality circles as necessary. Sometimes an area identified as in need of intervention is rather complex and no quick fixes or immediately obvious solutions can be implemented right away. In such instances, the creation of a "quality circle" to address the issue can be helpful. For example, one institution identified its financial aid and recruitment scale as an obvious target for intervention, but they were not sure how or where to start to change the financial aid picture on campus. So they created a quality circle comprising the director and a frontline staff member in financial aid; staff members from the billing office, the registrar's office, and admissions; a faculty member from the admissions committee; and two students. This group conducted focus groups, interviewed students as they came into the financial aid office, surveyed students more specifically about financial aid, and then tried to identify more comprehensively and specifically the areas in need of change. Then they brainstormed ways of meeting these challenges, worked up a plan that they proposed to the president's cabinet, and implemented changes the following year. Quality circles are not necessary for every area in need of intervention, but where there is a considerable amount of interaction with other areas of campus and where the challenges are complex, quality circles can be an excellent way of addressing the needs. Quality circles represent collaborative problem solving at its best.

Use SSI data for long-range planning. Not everything identified as a high priority can be fixed in a short amount of time. Some issues are complex, involving personnel, policies, budget priorities, and a significant investment of time and money. We recommend that issues that cannot be addressed within one year become part of the strategic plan. In this way, they do not get lost in the shuffle or put off from year to year due to lack of funds. By intentionally including high-priority areas in the strategic plan, institutions will be able to have the most impact on students' perceptions over the long run. And because strategic plans are supposed to reflect an intentional effort to improve institutional effectiveness and meet goals over a five- to ten-year period, what better way to focus that plan than around the issues that most dramatically affect students?

Assessing student satisfaction is not the only way to improve an institution's effectiveness. However, utilizing student satisfaction data is one of the best ways to get input from students about their perceptions of the quality they are receiving at a particular institution. Using that information along with other forms of assessment enables an institution of higher education to plan interventions that can have a significant and positive impact on the campus environment.

References

Juillerat, S. "Investigating a Two-Dimensional Approach to the Assessment of Student Satisfaction: Validation of the Student Satisfaction Inventory." Unpublished doctoral dissertation, Temple University, 1995.

Juillerat, S., and Schreiner, L. "The Role of Student Satisfaction in the Assessment of Institutional Effectiveness." *Assessment Update*, 1996, 8(1), 8–9.

Schreiner, L., and Juillerat, S. *The Student Satisfaction Inventory*. Iowa City, Iowa: Noel/Levitz Centers, 1993.

Stephanie Juillerat is associate professor of psychology at Wesley College, Dover, Delaware, and Laurie A. Schreiner is professor of psychology at Eastern College, St. Davids, Pennsylvania.

Using Classroom-Based Assessment for General Education

Ann-Janine Morey

This author describes how a faculty committee uses core courses themselves as indicators of successful student learning in a core curriculum. The committee reviews course syllabi for appropriate learning objectives as well as instructors' reports identifying assessment methods, findings, and use of findings to make improvements. Courses that fail to meet the committee's criteria are excluded from the core curriculum. From Assessment Update 11:5. For a listing of hallmarks illustrated in this article see the matrix on page 8.

At Southern Illinois University at Carbondale (SIUC) we have adapted the classroom-based assessment reported by Walvoord, Bardes, and Denton (1998) and have found it to be a valuable tool for both program evaluation and assessment.

As with most universities and colleges, SIUC's general education program, the University Core Curriculum, is not a degree-granting program. Core requirements consist of forty-one hours of arts and sciences courses that provide the supporting fabric for the major. In creating our assessment, we have tried to take into account several features of the Core Curriculum that create a challenge to meaningful assessment. One of these features is the sheer volume of students and faculty involved in core courses. Faculty have academic unit appointments and they offer core

courses at the discretion of the academic unit. In fall 1998, 739 instructors were delivering core courses. Of these, 51 percent were graduate as-
sistants and 32 percent were tenured or tenure-track faculty.

Another feature is our student body itself. We serve more than eigh-
teen thousand students each semester. Fully 65 percent of SIUC under-
graduates are transfer students, and most of what they transfer is general
education courses. Thus, any effort at general education assessment nec-
essarily means that if transfer students are in the pool, we are assessing
their total educational experience, not just the benefits of our particular
program. Finally, our four-year students do not take their core courses in
any particular order. The ideal is that they complete Foundation Skills
courses prior to the end of the sophomore year, but no stop is placed on
their enrollment should they fail to meet this expectation. Student enrollment is also defined by course sufficiency and student preferences. Students take what they can when it's available and when they please. There
is no predictable sequence of courses into which we might tap for an assessment snapshot of developing or completed outcome skills.

With these variables in mind, we designed classroom-based assessment
that offers multiple snapshots of ongoing student learning and evaluative
oversight of program goals. Our assessment establishes a portfolio for
every Core Curriculum course and through this process the courses themselves become the assessment indicators.

Methods and Results

Every instructor in the Core Curriculum is expected to assess student
learning outcomes in his or her core course on a regular basis. Learning
outcomes for each course are established by each delivering academic
unit, and we expect instructors of multiple sections of the same core
course to be teaching toward and assessing the same outcomes. We expect the learning outcomes established by each unit to speak directly to
program and area goals. To report our assessment, we have established a
longitudinal portfolio for each core course that documents this assessment and keeps current course materials on file. The Core Curriculum

Executive Council reviews these portfolios, evaluating both the course and the assessment report. There are now ninety-two courses in our Core Curriculum; we had documented assessment for sixty-nine of them as of fall 1998.

We review the syllabus for student learning outcomes and evaluate whether the learning objectives meet the goals established for the Core Curriculum. If the student learning objectives approved for that course meet core goals, if the instructor's assessment report documents the use of appropriate indicators for measuring student learning outcomes, and if the results of the assessment are being used to improve the course, we give that course a successful rating for meeting core goals. We provide both written and numerical feedback to the academic unit and we review subsequent assessment reports in light of our previous recommendations for improvement and in light of instructors' comments to us. Thus the feedback loop works at both the unit and program levels. In addition, we report our findings to the Campus-Wide Assessment Committee (CWAC), which completes the feedback loop at the institutional level. Thus, as Walvoord, Bardes, and Denton (1998, p. 10) comment, "if a teacher examines her students' performance using the PTA scores and changes her pedagogy accordingly, the department and institution need to know that such assessment is taking place, but they do not need to know actual scores or to tell the teacher what to do."

In this spirit, then, our Core Curriculum Executive Council is using core courses themselves as indicators of successful student learning in the Core Curriculum by creating a primary trait scale for assessing the course-as-indicator. When we report our findings to the CWAC, we provide two charts: one that specifies primary traits for course evaluation and another that specifies the relationship of course indicators and primary traits to core goals.

Accordingly, we reported that 73 percent of our courses have documented student learning outcomes that are congruent with core goals and reported using multiple measures, although 37 percent of these courses still need some improvement in how they are documenting or carrying out assessment. Another 26 percent of core courses are having trouble with assessment, including 3 percent whose instructors provided no information about student learning outcomes at all. We also reported that 91 percent of the courses in the areas of multicultural and interdisciplinary studies were satisfying core goal 5, "Enhance understanding and appreciation of diverse cultures and environments." Conversely, we found that we had no information about how many core courses satisfied goal 6, "Prepare students for ethical and responsible citizenship," because we failed to identify a primary trait to record this feature. Needless to say, we have revised our primary trait chart.

To offset the abstractness of this big-picture report, and to give the CWAC a flavor of the student outcomes assessments in each portfolio, we provide specific snapshots of the kinds of assessment evidence we are seeing. In our fall 98 report, we highlighted assessment reports from the philosophy, physics, sociology, English, chemistry, and mathematics departments.

In English 205 (enrollment: 97 in four sections), for example, an English department review team used teaching evaluations (indirect indicators) and sample student portfolios, holistically scored, to report assessment for this course. The team found that the two instructors involved got very different teaching evaluations, which suggested that either one of the instructors needed some assistance or perhaps the Department of English needed to rethink some of its teaching assignments. According to the portfolio analysis, 80 percent of the students in two of the four sections showed a satisfactory ability to use critical concepts, critical terminology, and textual support in their writing. The Department of English will be revising the course description and working more closely with instructors to obtain greater congruence in outcomes from section to section.

Sociology 215 (enrollment: 335 in five sections) used competence-based assessment by identifying final exam questions (objective and essay) that spoke to particular student-learning objectives: grasping concepts, historical and demographic information, and sociological theory. Between 75 and 85 percent of the students in each section responded correctly to questions. In one section, students performed less well on applying sociological concepts; in another they were weaker on grasping concepts. The instructor of the second section crowed about an 85 percent success rate on grasping concepts because she had deliberately emphasized these in class.

The reporting instructor of Mathematics 110 registered frustration over assessment results. Several assignments (group labs, exams, homework, and papers) were scored using a primary trait scale correlated with student learning objectives. The learning objective that gave students the most trouble was development of a proper mathematical vocabulary. More than half showed no improvement on the exam. Performance distributions along with interaction in class also indicated that some students were struggling with writing in mathematics. The instructor decided to include more math vocabulary exercises in all class assignments and to spend more time developing a class culture oriented to group learning activities that will improve the writing and conceptual component of student performance.

Discussion and Conclusion

As a result of our assessment process, instructors and academic units are making changes in their core courses that are designed to improve student learning. At the program level, courses that cannot provide satisfactory assessment reports, or that are having difficulty delivering the course in congruence with program goals, will be excluded from the Core Curriculum. As a result of assessment, nine courses have been put on warning and two courses have been placed on pending cancellation. Because the Core Curriculum is a source of many student credit hours, most academic units have been willing to talk about improvement rather than see a course eliminated.

Our assessment process has also resulted in further refinement of the campus Assessment Plan. We decided to have the academic units and instructors delivering the courses define appropriate student learning outcomes for their core courses. As long as the stated student learning objectives supported core and area goals (which were defined by the Core Curriculum Executive Council), we were satisfied that meaningful assessment could occur. The benefit of this move was that the council reviewers were not expected to read through a complicated layer of goals-and-objectives statements in order to comprehend what was happening for students in the classroom. In addition, this move empowered faculty, who all too often view assessment as an externally imposed burden.

Our classroom-based assessment has not been without problems. Members of SIUC's CWAC initially were uneasy that they were not seeing student learning outcomes reported directly from a conventional programwide assessment, as one might expect for the major. Core faculty complained that this assessment was more demanding than they were expected to supply for the major. This complaint stemmed in part from the issue of faculty buy-in. Needless to say, we have learned a good deal about tone in this process of assessment feedback. Our strategy has been patience and repetition — we are trying to make sure that all core faculty understand the importance of articulating student learning objectives and the relationship of those objectives to program goals and assessment.

Another problem has been the labor-intensive nature of our assessment start-up. To establish a baseline portfolio for each course, the provost provided reading stipends for the Core Curriculum Executive Council, and we spent a summer reading all of the portfolios collected during one academic year. Even with the incentive of the stipend, council members who participated in this start-up found themselves weary of assessment by the conclusion and a bit peevish when we commenced the next series of readings. But having established the baseline, we are now preparing to move to a selective rotational reading, which will make the council's annual task more manageable. For example, we would like to focus on interdisciplinary studies courses. Our first assessments indicate that instructors are having some difficulty aligning these courses with the area goals, and it is possible that we need to do a better job of relating this area of the program to faculty expertise and interests. This is another way in which we anticipate that assessment will result in programmatic changes. Finally, we discovered that the drive toward quantifiable, documented improvement in student performance leaves out a crucial variable—the student. The instructor of Mathematics 110 was joined by a number of other instructors in commenting that one significant barrier to improved student learning performance is poor class attendance. This often-repeated comment from our faculty about student attendance and motivation as elements in learning suggests that a new phase of assessment will need to take account of the critical element of student responsibility for learning outcomes. Such consideration could be helpful to those of us who are negotiating the tricky territory of general education assessment.

Reference

Walvoord, B. E., Bardes, B., and Denton, J. "Closing the Feedback Loop in Classroom-Based Assessment." *Assessment Update*, 1998, *10*(5), 1–2, 10.

Ann-Janine Morey, formerly director of the University Core Curriculum at Southern Illinois University at Carbondale, is associate dean for program development in the College of Arts and Letters at James Madison University.

Assessment and Program Review: Linking Two Processes

Dwight Smith, Douglas Eder

In 1998 a statewide program review process in Illinois was modified to include a requirement that institutions show how they are using findings from outcomes assessment to guide improvements of their programs. The authors describe how Southern Illinois University–Edwardsville has used a senior assignment—a scholarly engagement between a senior student and a professor that yields an assessable product of the student's learning—to address the new state requirement. From Assessment Update 13:1. For a listing of hallmarks illustrated in this article see the matrix on page 8.

Assessment and program review are two activities conducted in higher education to improve educational quality. Assessment, begun in the 1980s, is used in a variety of ways to improve teaching and student learning and can be employed in the classroom or at the unit level.

Program review as described in this article has functioned on a statewide basis in Illinois since the mid-1970s as a result of a state statute establishing the Illinois Board of Higher Education (IBHE). Assessment and program review function at different time intervals, but each poses similar questions regarding teaching and student learning (for example, What are the characteristics of a powerful learning environment?). When assessment and program review are linked, the academic unit can function like the learning organization described by Senge (1990) and can provide insight into the improvement of educational quality.

Authentic Assessment Through a Senior Assignment

At Southern Illinois University–Edwardsville (SIUE), we define a Senior Assignment (SRA) as a scholarly engagement between a senior student and a dedicated professor (or professors), embedded in the ways of knowing of the discipline, that results in a product. The product can be an artistic performance, public speech, technical design, written thesis, gallery presentation, or a combination of these with other forms of expression. Ideal SRAs have several major properties, only three of which are described here. First, the SRA is a natural, visible product of the student's learning. That product makes student performance and the curriculum behind it assessable, usually by employing primary trait analysis (Walvoord and Anderson, 1998) to compare actual student achievement with preset goals and standards for baccalaureate graduates. Second, really good SRAs reflect the context of the discipline that produced them; that is, they reveal not just students' mastery of the discipline but also their judgment about it. Through the SRA, students are asked to demonstrate qualities similar to those exhibited by faculty in the discipline. SRAs put students in situations required of practitioners, thus assessing them authentically (Wiggins, 1993). Third, by asking students to investigate and demonstrate the natural but messy business of how a conclusion actually comes into being in their discipline, SRAs require students to become participants in their education. In the same way that an airplane cockpit flight simulator both teaches and assesses in authentic, supervised situations, so does the SRA both engage and assess the student authentically. To use Steve Ehrmann's term, the SRA functions as an academic simulator (Ehrmann, 1998).

Program Review

SIUE follows an eight-year program review cycle established by the Illinois Board of Higher Education. During the cycle, similar programs (for example, sciences, engineering, business, education) at the 12 state universities are reviewed simultaneously. That is, in a given year all engineering programs at public universities are reviewed. For the review, all are asked to address the questions and criteria that appear in Table 1.

The variety of data used to answer these questions is analyzed by faculty, program chairs, deans, and the provost. Faculty governance and other relevant constituencies are thoroughly involved. The full program review process, with academic and administrative components, takes approximately two years. Data used to document each criterion are indicated in Table 2.

Of note is the use of the Senior Assignment as a quality indicator. The importance of this type of assessment in program review has become prominent as the Illinois Board of Higher Education has redefined the process. This change, begun during the 1998–99 academic year, asks the following questions:

1. What has the program done since the last review?
2. What opportunities for program improvement have been identified?
3. How have assessment results been used?
4. What has been learned from the review?

As Question 3 suggests, assessment is now an important element of the program review process and informs the answers to Question 4.

The use of the Senior Assignment in program review has led to faculty insights into SIUE program strengths and areas for improvement. Some of the strengths identified across the university include disciplinary knowledge, student analysis and problem solving, sensitivity to diversity, and critical thinking within the discipline. Areas identified for overall improvement include written and oral communication, research method-

Table 1. Program Review Criteria and Questions for Illinois State Universities

Program Review Criteria	*Questions*
Student demand	Do the credit hours, enrollments, or degree production of this program differ significantly from statewide or institutional averages?
Occupational demand	What are the occupational objectives of students enrolled in the program? Do state employment projections in occupations related to the program show adequate job openings for graduates? Is there a need for the program based on occupational demand?
Centrality to instructional mission	Is the program central to the instructional mission of the university? To what extent does the program provide instructional support to students and faculty in other programs?
Breadth	Is there sufficient student interest and demand for all courses, specializations, options, and minors offered as part of the program? Are faculty and resources deployed productively?
Success of graduates	Do graduates of the program report appropriate rates of job placement or progress in further education? Do current students and alumni report satisfaction with the program?
Costs	Has there been a significant increase or decrease in the unit costs of the program? Do the costs of the program deviate significantly from statewide average costs in the discipline? Can any deviation be corrected within existing resources?
Quality	Is the program achieving its objectives? Are faculty qualified and productive? Is the curriculum consistent with program objectives and up to date? Are academic support resources (including library, laboratory, and equipment/materials) adequate and up-to-date? Are high standards for student performance maintained? Do students achieve their academic and career objectives?
Productivity	What steps have been taken to improve the quality and productivity of this program? What investment or cost savings (annual and five-year projection) resulted from the review of this program?

Source: Illinois Board of Higher Education, 1993, pp. IV-6—IV-7.

ology, and quantitative analysis. Findings acquired in this way rise above the level of anecdote and, given their alignment with faculty priorities, usually result in action (for example, replacing an old required course with a new one or adding new emphasis to an existing course). Specific SIUE assessment findings, program by program, can be found at <http://www.siue.edu/~deder/assess/index.html>.

Implications of Linking Assessment and Program Review

One lesson learned from linking assessment to program review is that professors who annually examine assessment results and take action based

Table 2. Data Used to Document Each Program Review Criterion in Illinois State Universities

Program Review Criteria	Data
Student demand and costs	• Annual enrollment and degrees granted
	• Program costs in comparison to statewide mean
Occupational demand	• Department of Labor projections (state and federal)
	• Professional organization projections
Centrality and breadth	• Service loads by discipline
	• General education courses offered and enrollment
Success of graduates	• Baccalaureate surveys one, five, and ten years out
	• Faculty anecdotes on student placement
	• Certification and licensing pass rates
Quality	• Faculty Program Review Committee report
	• External reviewers
	• Program director's questionnaire
	• Senior Assignment
	• Surveys one, five, and ten years out
	• Faculty teaching, research, and service awards
	• Current student surveys and interviews
	• Accreditation reviews
	• Alumni advisory boards
Productivity	• Student time to degree
	• Faculty research and service productivity
	• Curriculum revision
	• Student recruitment
	• Degrees granted
Statewide analysis by IBHE	• Dependent on issues

on them continually improve student learning. Assessment is generally a formative process over which faculty have considerable control. As Sheila Tobias (1992) observed, programs that share a sense of unity and engage in regular, serious, shared assessments of student learning tend to be more successful and effective. This becomes evident in program review, which tends to be a summative process. Faculty in a unified program begin to see program review not as a time for summative judgment but as an opportunity to consider more publicly their efforts to improve student learning. Faculty in such a program, by assembling and presenting a case for serious peer review, foster what Boyer (1990) calls "scholarship of teaching." The frequency of program review—once every eight years in Illinois—allows time for improvements to be identified, made, tested, and reassessed. Changes in curriculum and teaching require time to implement if they are to have a measurable effect on students. Linking the two processes of assessment and program review is helpful to faculty, students, and administrators as they consider ways to improve educational quality.

References

Boyer, E. L. *Scholarship Reconsidered*. San Francisco: Jossey-Bass, 1990.

Ehrmann, S. C. *Information to Action: Asking Good Questions, Generating Useful Answers, and Communicating Well*. Cincinnati, Ohio: AAHE Assessment Conference, 1998.

Illinois Board of Higher Education. *IBHE RAMP Manual*. Springfield: Illinois Board of Higher Education, 1993.

Senge, P. M. *The Fifth Discipline: The Art and Practice of the Learning Organization*. New York: Doubleday, 1990.

Tobias, S. *Revitalizing Undergraduate Science: Why Some Things Work and Most Don't*. Tucson, Ariz.: Research Corporation, 1992.

Walvoord, B. E., and Anderson, V. J. *Effective Grading: A Tool for Learning and Assessment*. San Francisco: Jossey-Bass, 1998.

Wiggins, G. "Assessment: Authenticity, Context, and Validity." *Phi Delta Kappan*, Nov. 1993, pp. 200–214.

Dwight Smith is assistant provost for planning at Southern Illinois University at Edwardsville. Douglas Eder is Emerson Scholar at Hamilton College.

Assessment UPdate
COLLECTIONS

Assessment Update Collections provide readers with information on specific areas of assessment—gathered together for the first time in a single, easy-to-use booklet format. Specially selected by editor Trudy W. Banta from the rich archives of *Assessment Update*, the articles in these booklets represent the best thinking on various topics and are chosen to ensure that readers have information that is relevant and comprehensive and illustrates effective practice. **Ordering information:** Each booklet costs $14.95 and can be ordered by calling 888.378.2537 or visiting our Web site at www.josseybass.com. Want to order additional copies of this booklet? Call Lora Templeton at 415.782.3127 for information on our bulk discounts.

Portfolio Assessment This booklet's articles explore how portfolios, including Web-based portfolios, have been used at various institutions to assess and improve programs in general education, the major, advising, and overall institutional effectiveness. They describe ways portfolios can be scored, students' perspectives on portfolios, how portfolios changed the faculty culture at one college, and more. 80 pages ISBN 0-7879-7286-X

Community College Assessment Nowhere is the need for assessment methods of demonstrated value felt more strongly than at the community college. This booklet gathers together for the first time some of the best illustrations of good practice available, addressing such issues as evaluating transfer success, assessing employer needs, community and technical college students' perceptions of student engagement, corporate partnerships in assessment, and much more. 74 pages ISBN 0-7879-7287-8

Hallmarks of Effective Outcomes Assessment This booklet brings together the best guidance and practices from *Assessment Update* to illustrate time-tested principles for all aspects of assessment from planning and implementing to sustaining and improving assessment efforts over time. Useful for those new to assessment as well as experienced practitioners, it details the specific hallmarks required for the success of any assessment program—from leadership and staff development to the assessment of processes as well as outcomes, ongoing communication among constituents, and more. 72 pages ISBN 0-7879-7288-6

About the Editor: Trudy W. Banta is vice chancellor for planning and institutional improvement at Indiana University-Purdue University Indianapolis and editor of the bimonthly *Assessment Update: Progress, Trends, and Practices in Higher Education*. She has written or edited 10 published volumes on assessment, including *Assessment Essentials*, with Catherine Palomba (Jossey-Bass, 1999) and *Building a Scholarship of Assessment* (Jossey-Bass, 2002). Banta has been honored for her work by the National Council on Measurement in Education, the American Association for Higher Education, the American Productivity and Quality Center, and the Association for Institutional Research.